DISCOVERING WHO YOU REALLY ARE

You Have The Power To Transform Your Life

Jill Patton

Table of Contents

Chapter 1:

10 Life Skills You Need To Have

<u>What is life?</u>

Nobody has ever fully exhausted the explanation of what life entails. It is a mystery that hitherto has never been completely unraveled. It is an examination where every candidate has a different question paper and the marking scheme is adhered to ruthlessly.

We can learn from the experience of our predecessors how they managed to meander through the obstacles of life. They must have a few life hack tricks that are indispensable in making our life easier. Here are ten necessary life skills to ace the game of life:

1. <u>Assertiveness.</u>

It is the skill of being honest and transparent with yourself and the people you interact with. The quality of honesty is rare making it thoroughly sought for. Nobody wants to deal with dishonest people because they can sink their boat of success.

Assertiveness or lack of it distinguishes nobles from commoners. It works magic to those who practice it. People consider them reliable and the future calls out to them to secure it.

2. <u>Integrity.</u>

Integrity is a wider scope of assertiveness. Apart from being honest, people of integrity uphold a higher standard of morality. They have hard stances against vices of every nature and cannot compromise on anything that hurts their belief.

As a life skill, integrity secures you the moral authority to condemn societal ills. It becomes even more important to build a reputation of integrity if you are a public figure. Furthermore, integrity protects its holders from the effects of vices like corruption.

3. Critical thinkers.

Critical thinking involves deeper reasoning of the motives behind actions, the consequences of choices, and the impact of alternative decisions we could make.

It is important to develop critical thinking to evaluate matters before arriving at conclusions. There is little to no chance of having regrets if you have critical thinking.

4. Self-love.

Self-love is caring for yourself as you do others. It does not lean to selfishness but according to yourself an equal treatment as the people you interact with.

Do not overlook self-love because it is a skill that few people have mastered. Those who lack it suffer from a bruised ego and low self-esteem.

5. Interpersonal skills.

They are skills that enable one to interact properly with people they meet. Personal relationships have reduced drastically due to advancements in technology. People prefer virtual meetings to physical ones.

You need to stand out by being unique and embrace interpersonal skills. You will be able to make friendships faster and build a network of trustworthy friends.

6. Self-confidence.

How can other people have confidence in you if you doubt yourself? Self-confidence is key in winning the trust of other people. You need to exude confidence in the values you believe for other people to follow suit.

In a business world, believe in yourself and the products or services you offer for clients to value your input. Self-confidence is not pride but a demonstration of competence.

7. Creativity.

It is the ability to think outside the ordinary and come up with original suggestions and ideas. Creativity is limitless and does not discriminate against age or gender. Everyone is creative at their level. It is their complexity to wind simple ideas into great sustainable ventures that increase the value of creative people.

Creativity augments the value a person brings to the table. It is a necessary life skill that raises the quality of life from a personal level.

8. Arbitration skills.

Arbitration is the act of being an impartial judge in a conflict between two or more parties. Since conflicts are inevitable, it comes in handy to unite the warring groups. How would life be without people to justly arbitrate conflicts?

It is an important life skill because it makes one a peacemaker. Moreover, arbiters largely live peaceful lives because they have learned from the mistakes of those they help.

9. Analytical skills.

A critical analysis of situations is necessary to make informed decisions. Analytical skills enable one to distinguish right from wrong. They can decipher deception from afar even when it is properly concealed.

There comes a time when we are left alone without guidance and find our way around unfamiliar territories. We require strong analytical skills to remain afloat.

10. Fast thinking.

There is often a lot of emphasis on correct thinking and logic and we forget how fast we need to do it. It is not enough that we can arrive at correct conclusions. It is useless if we cannot do it faster to save an already worse situation.

Fast thinking is a skill only taught in the school of life and not classrooms. Learn to develop fast solutions to problems because time makes all the difference.

In conclusion, these ten life skills are just a few from a pool of many that are essential for survival. They make life easier for all those who have them.

Chapter 2:

Six Steps To Create A Vision For Your Life

Let me ask you this question, have you ever felt so stuck in where you are? That feeling when you wanna move and be somewhere else because you don't like where you are but you don't know where to go either? That is the worst feeling ever, right?

Creating a vision for your life will save you from being stuck and lost. These visions are the pictures you create about the life that you want to live.

Here are 6 Steps To Start Envisioning Your Future
Step number 1, identify what matters to you. Ask yourself, "what's really important to me?". Is it health? Career? Wealth? Relationships? Passion? Time? It could be a balance of all those things. What legacy would you want to leave in this world? Identifying what truly matters to you and what you really value gives you a destination of where you want to be. Having these in mind, all your plans and decisions will be centered towards your destination.

Next step is thinking ahead, but at the same time, also believing that it is already happening for you right now. Be specific in chasing what you want, don't just simply limit yourself to what you think is socially acceptable. If you limit your choices to what seems to be reasonable, you are disconnecting yourself from your true potentialDon't compromise.. Be as audacious as you want to be, it's your own life anyway! You have all the right to dream as big as you want. Talk as if your dreams are happening right now. When you have this big dream, you won't settle for less just because it is what's available at the moment.

Step number 3, assess and challenge your motives. Ask yourself, "is this the kind of life I wanna live because it is what the society is expecting from me?", "am I doing this because this is what everybody else is doing?" Knowing your real motive towards your visions will help you uncover what your heart really desires. You might even be surprised by what you'll discover within you when you remove all the layers that the world has planted in you.

Next step, be sure that your visions are aligned with a purpose. You don't need to know exactly what your life purpose is, unless you've already figured that out somehow. But your visions should be relevant to how you want your life to be. For example, if your goal is to maintain your mental well-being, your vision might be to live your life peacefully while focusing on the things that truly matter. Your vision should serve you the purpose into making your life as pleasing as you want it.

Step number 5 is to be accountable for your own visions. Don't tie your visions into someone else's hands. Your visions may involve direct impact to others but make sure that your visions are not dependent on other people. Why? Because people, just like the seasons, change. People come and go. The version of the people in your life right now is not how they will be for the rest of their lives. And so are you. Hold these visions in your own hands and make sure you execute it diligently and faithfully.

Last step is to make room for changes. You will grow as a person, that is a fact. You won't have the same exact priorities all through your life. And that's okay. Whatever you want to change into is valid. Your goals and dreams are all valid. Changes are inevitable so don't be afraid if you have to change what's working for you from time to time.

While you are in the process of making your life's visions, be as creative as you can. Although the world is not a wish-granting factory, remember that through your hard work and perseverance, nothing is really impossible. You have everything in you to achieve your goals and live through your visions. You just need to be clear about what you really want or where you wanna be.

Remember that our days in this world are limited. We won't be able to live our lives to the fullest if we are just merely existing or living by default. We are humans. And as humans, we have the power to lead the life we truly desire. Sometimes, we are just one decision away from it. I hope what we've talked about today will not just inspire you to make your life's visions but also help you to understand why you need to make them. You deserve a kind of life that will excite you to wake up everyday because you know what you are waking up for.

Chapter 3:

5 Ways To Focus on Creating Positive Actions

Only a positive person can lead a healthy life. Imagine waking up every day feeling like you are ready to face the day's challenges and you are filled with hope about life. That is something an optimist doesn't have to imagine because they already feel it every day. Also, scientifically, it is proven that optimistic people have a lower chance of dying because of a stress-caused disease. Although positive thinking will not magically vanish all your problems, it will make them seem more manageable and somewhat not a big deal.

All you have to do is focus on the positive side of life. It is not necessarily true that people with a positive mindset always get disappointed. Positivity is like a breath of fresh air for us. Looking at the bright side of things has its advantages, and it has its very own benefits. So, positive energy is an essential factor to produce in oneself to make them more efficient in the ways of life. They tend to focus on all the good things and push aside all the wrong things, making them love everything they do.

1. Think Positively

Positive thinking is what leads to positive actions, actions that affect you and the people around you. When you think positively, your actions show

how positive you are. You can create positive thinking by focusing on the good in life, even if it may feel tiny thing to feel happy about because when you once learn to be satisfied with minor things, you would think that you no longer feel the same amount of stress as before and now you would feel freer. This positive attitude will always find the good in everything, and life would seem much easier than before. You then become the person you once imagined yourself to be, just by thinking positively about it. So, make sure to process those positive thoughts thoroughly for better results or action.

2. Be Grateful

Being grateful for the things you have contributed a lot to your positive behavior. Gratitude has proven to reduce stress and improve self-esteem. Think of the things you are grateful for; for example, if someone gives you good advice, then be thankful to them, for if someone has helped you with something, then be grateful to them, by being grateful about minor things, you feel more optimistic about life, you feel that good things have always been coming to you. Studies show that making down a list of things you are grateful for during hard days helps you survive tough times. Also, be thankful to yourself for making achievements that you wanted. It makes you feel positive about yourself and makes your confidence boost through you. You have to make sure that you know what it is to be thankful for. Be grateful to someone for all the right reasons, and you will feel positive.

3. Laugh Through Situations

A person laughing always looks like a happy person. Studies have shown that laughter lowers stress, anxiety, and depression. Open yourself up to humor, permit yourself to laugh even if forced because even a forced laugh can improve your mood. Laughter lightens the mood and makes problems seem more manageable. Your laughter is contagious, and it may even enhance the perspective of the people around us. Smiling is free therapy. You have to pass an approving smile and make someone's day up.

4. Don't Blame Yourself For The Things You Can't Control

People with depression or anxiety are always their jailers; being harsh on themselves will only cause pain, negativity, and insecurity. So try to be soft with yourself, give yourself a positive talk regularly; it has proven to affect a person's actions. A positive word to yourself can influence your ability to regulate your feelings and thoughts. The positivity you carry in your brain is expressed through your actions, and who doesn't loves an optimistic person. Instead of blaming yourself, you can think differently, like "I will do better next time" or "I can fix this." Being optimistic about the complicated situation can lead your brain to find a solution to that problem.

5. Start Your Day with A dose of Positivity

When you wake up, it is good to do something positive in the morning, which mentally freshens you. You can start the day by reading a positive quote about life and understand the meaning of that quote, and you may feel an overwhelming feeling after letting the meaning set. Everybody loves a good song, so start by listening to a piece of music that gives you positive vibes, that gives you hope, and motivation for the day. You can also share your positivity by being nice to someone or doing something nice for someone; you will find that you feel thrilled and positive by making someone else happy.

Conclusion

Indeed, we can not just start thinking positively overnight, but we have to push ourselves more every time to improve. Surround yourself with brightness, good people, and a positive mindset—a good combination for a good life.

Chapter 4:

Never Stop Even If Someone Tells You To

Your brain works in mysterious ways, and it has a way of complying with negative things much faster than the positives. It is a part of human nature to not accept things that make one feel good about themselves because if they do, they are termed "narcissistic" or "self-obsessed."

With the way things have taken a turn, the world has become a much more competitive place, and one needs to shoot for the moon to land among the stars. In a world so fast, if you can come up with unique and different ideas from others, not only do you stand out, but it also gives rise to the opposition. This is where people start discouraging you and telling you how you are not good enough. This is where your idea gets lost in their judgment, and you start doubting yourself and question if everything is worth it or not.

A million people out there are ready to step on you and crush your self-esteem and confidence because that is what they strive for. If you give them the strength and ability to take that away from you, it is in your hands. One of the strongest weapons one has is self-confidence which can take them to places they had only dreamt of, but if it is crushed, all that is ahead is failure and insecurities. As Johann Wolfgang von Goethe said, "As soon as you trust yourself, you will know how to live."

The path of success is never doubting yourself when someone tells you "No" and moving forward by trusting yourself instead of putting it in their judgment. If people's opinions measured success, great people like Albert Einstein wouldn't have made history. He failed school at the age of 16 and was told that he would always be a failure but imagine if he had stopped then, who would have developed the theory of relativity? Probably no one!

The truth is that while you might be good in one thing, you will always lack in one thing or another and you will be made felt like you are a failure. It is important not to listen to people when they tell you to stop because you cannot do it. You can! And you should not believe otherwise. Imagine if Einstein was asked to write a love song? Or Rihanna to come up with a theory of relativity? We wouldn't have had a world-class singer or a physicist. Thus, it is important to figure out your strengths and work towards polishing them. Move on with things and put in that belief that you can do it. Because trust us, if you tell yourself, you can do it. No one telling you otherwise will matter!

Chapter 5:

It's Okay To Feel Uncertain

We are surrounded by a world that has endless possibilities. A world where no two incidents can predict the other. A realm where we are a slave to the unpredictable future and its repercussions.

Everyone has things weighing on their mind. Some of us know it and some of us keep carrying these weights unknowingly.

The uncertainty of life is the best gift that you never wanted. But when you come to realize the opportunities that lie at every uneven corner are worth living for.

Life changes fast, sometimes in our favor and sometimes not much. But life always has a way to balance things out. We only need to find the right approach to make things easier for us and the ones around us.

Everyone gets tested once in a while, but we need to find ways to cope with life when things get messy.

The worst thing the uncertainty of life can produce is the fear in your heart. The fear to never know what to expect next. But you can never let fear rule you.

To worry about the future ahead of us is pointless. So change the question from 'What if?' to 'What will I do if.'

If you already have this question popping up in your brain, this means that you are already getting the steam off.

You don't need to fear the uncertain because you can never wreck your life in any such direction from where there is no way back.

The uncertainty of life is always a transformation period to make you realize your true path. These uncertainties make you realize the faults you might have in your approach to things.

You don't need to worry about anything unpredictable and unexpected because not everything is out of your control every time. Things might not happen in a way you anticipated but that doesn't mean you cannot be prepared for it.

There are a lot of things that are in your control and you are well researched and well equipped to go around events. So use your experience to do the damage control.

Let's say you have a pandemic at your hand which you couldn't possibly predict, but that doesn't mean you cannot do anything to work on its effects. You can raise funds for the affected population. You can try to find new ways to minimize unemployment. You can find alternate ways to keep the economy running and so on.

Deal with your emotions as you cannot get carried away with such events being driven by your feelings.

Don't avoid your responsibilities and don't delay anything. You have to fulfill every task expected of you because you were destined to do it. The results are not predetermined on a slate but you can always hope for the best be the best version of yourself no matter how bad things get.

Life provides us with endless possibilities because when nothing is certain, anything is possible. So be your own limit.

Chapter 6:

Meditate to Rewire Your Brain for Happiness

Suppose you've ever read the book Bridge to Terabithia (or seen the movie). In that case, you are familiar with Terabithia – an imaginary world that the main characters, Jesse and Leslie, create as a haven. It is somewhere they can go to be free from the cares and worries of the world.

Meditation has given me a Terabithia. I have created a clearing of calm and tranquility that I can enter into within seconds whenever I feel the need. I have a refuge no matter where I am or what I am doing. The worries of the world no longer threaten me. Except this mental place isn't imaginary, and it isn't populated with trolls and wild creatures – it is as real as the world we live in.

Since starting my meditation habit, my brain has been rewired for happiness, peace, and success. Here are just a few of the benefits:

I rarely become angry.

I find happiness in unexpected places.

I form deeper relationships and build friendships more easily.

However, by far, the largest benefit is that a deep, serene calm and peace is slowly permeating into every area of my life. At first, meditating felt unusual – like I was stepping out of normal life and doing something that most people find strange. I soon realized, however, that this wasn't true – millions of people meditate, and many successful people attribute part of their success to meditation.

Oprah Winfrey, Hugh Jackman, Richard Branson, Paul McCartney, Angelina Jolie… Any of these names sound familiar? All of these are famous meditators.

This list alone is powerful, but maybe you need a little more convincing that meditation is something you should try.

Michael Jordan, Kobe Bryant, Misty-May Trainor, and Derek Jeter are just a few successful athletes who rely on meditation to get them in the zone.

Rupert Murdoch, Russell Simons, and Arianna Huffington all practice meditation.

Arnold Schwarzenegger and Eva Mendez are just a couple more celebrities that make meditation a daily habit.

Meditation Reduces Stress

Are you feeling the weight of the world on your shoulders? Meditation is incredibly effective at reducing stress and anxiety. One study found that mindfulness and zen-type meditations significantly reduce stress when practiced over a period of three months. Another study revealed that meditation reduces the density of brain tissue associated with anxiety and worrying. If you want your stress levels to plummet, meditation may be the answer.

Chapter 7:

Live A Long, Important Life

Do you think you are more capable to deal with the failure or the regret of not trying at all?

Are you living the life you want or the life everyone else wants for you?

Would you feel good spending your time on entertainment that might not last for long? Or would you feel good feeling like you are growing and have a better self of you to look at in the mirror?

Similarly, would like to live in the present or would you love to work for a better future?

Do you want money to dictate your life or do you want money to follow you where ever you go?

Would you prefer being tired or being broke?

Do you want to spend the rest of your life in this place where you and your parents were born? Or do you won't go around the world and find new possibilities in even the most remote places?

Would you rather risk it all or play it safe?

We are often presented with all these questions in our lifetime. Most people take these questions as a way to enter into your adulthood. The answers to these questions are meant to show you the actual meaning of life.

So what is Life? Life is not your parents, your work, your friends, your events, and your functions. It's within you and around you.

You should learn to live your life to the fullest. You should love to live your life for as long as you can with a happy body and a healthy mind.

A happy and healthy body and mind are important. Because you can only feel secure on a stable platform. You can only wish to stand on a platform where you know you can stay put for a long time.

There is nothing wrong with working eight or nine hours in your daily life. It's not unhealthy or anything. Working is what gives our life a purpose. Working is what keeps us active, moving, and motivated.

We have one life, and we have to make it matter. But the way we chose to do it is what matters the most. Our choices make us who we are rather than our actions.

The life we live is the epitome of our intentions and morals. We can be defined in a single word or a single phrase if we ever try. We don't need to analyze someone else, we just need to see ourselves in the mirror and we might be able to see right across the image.

The day we are able to do that, might be the day we have actually made a worthy human being of ourselves and have fulfilled our destiny.

If you are able to look at yourself and go through your whole life in the blink of an eye and cherish the memories as if you were right there at that moment. Believe me, you have had a long and important life to make you think of it all over again every day.

Chapter 8:

Treat Failure Like A Scientist

Have you ever studied the life of a scientist in general? Do you know what a scientist actually does? A scientist conducts experiments to study the true nature and the working of the universe.

Scientists have a strategy to work ahead. They perform the experiments and they get results. Some are in the favor of their original theory and some are against them.

But never do these results have a personal attachment to anything. The results are data points and each data point has an importance to the study.

The scientist cannot neglect any result whether it be a success or a total failure because it will make them realize the faults they made the first time and will eventually help them and others after them to take a better start or a better theory.

The same is the case with our lives. We have to understand the working philosophy of life and failures.

People get carried away with the smallest of setbacks. We get discouraged and demotivated by the smallest of things that might not even be that big a deal. But we are so used to making such a big deal out of every little hitch.

We get stuck in the pitfall that we create ourselves and never try to realize the true mercy or lesson that little moments of pain and failure might have taught us.

Failures leave a mark, that is for sure. But those marks don't have to be bad. Whether you make those marks a war wound or a scar is up to you.

You live life as you please. Other people do the same thing. But we are not all the same, and no one can say what is right and what is wrong. But there is a simple way to judge. Let's say we get a reward for doing something good and it makes us feel good.

But when we do something from the top of our head and we are not sure what impact it will have on others, the result will make it clear and will be a lesson for the rest of our lives.

Your intentions are always in the right place, but failures still get you. So failing is not fun, but it should be held against you. You had a reason for all of this and now you have a reason to not do the same thing again.

This result made you eliminate one small thing that made you look bad the first time. So you were able to remove one more spot from your bigger picture and now you are a better individual altogether.

Failure is simply a cost you have to pay on the way to being right. Your failures don't define you, but you can define your failures. You can either let it remain a failure or you can change it into a success story by sticking to the process of turning wrongs into rights. And you will go through this learning throughout your life.

Chapter 9:

How To Become A Morning Person

Our natural sleep/wake cycles are known as our circadian rhythm, and they can vary a lot from person to person. People fall into different groups, or chronotypes, depending on whether they feel most awake and alert in the morning, in the evening or somewhere in between.

No chronotype is inherently better or worse than another. There's nothing wrong with staying up late and sleeping in. "If that schedule fits with your lifestyle and your obligations, it's not necessary to change it."

The trouble comes when your late bedtime clashes with your early morning obligations. If you're regularly getting less than the recommended seven to nine hours of sleep a night, your health and well-being can suffer.

Unfortunately, we can't pick our chronotypes. Genetics plays a part in whether you identify as a night owl or a morning lark. Still, your habits and behaviours can reinforce those natural tendencies. And those habits aren't set in stone. "By making behavioural changes, you may be able to shift your sleep schedule preferences,"

How to reset your circadian rhythm? How, exactly, do you become more of a morning person?

Shift your bedtime: Count back from the time your alarm rings, aiming for a total of seven to nine hours a night. That will be your target bedtime — eventually. If you're used to turning in well after midnight, willing yourself to suddenly fall asleep at 10:00 p.m. is sure to backfire.

Aim to go to bed 15 or 20 minutes earlier than usual for a few days. Then push it back another 15 minutes for several more days. "It's important to adjust your sleep time gradually," she says.

Make it routine: A quiet bedtime routine is key to helping you fall asleep earlier. At least an hour before lights out, dim the lights and power down your electronics. Find something soothing to do, like taking a warm bath, reading a book or listening to a (not-too-stimulating) podcast. "Give yourself time to wind down and prepare your mind for bed."

Lighten up: "Our circadian rhythms are responsive to light and dark," Exposure to bright light first thing in the morning helps you feel more alert and also helps shift your internal rhythm toward an earlier wake time.

Natural light is the best, so get outside or open your bedroom window. If you can't get outside or your room is natural light-deprived, try a light therapy lamp that mimics the spectrum of natural light.

Make mornings more pleasant: Try to schedule something to look forward to in the morning so that getting up feels like less of a slog. Perhaps a hot cup of coffee, sipped in silence, and the daily crossword puzzle. Knowing that something pleasant awaits can help you take that first, painful step out of bed.

Move your alarm clock: Hitting snooze is all too tempting, so remove that option. Try putting your alarm clock across the room, so you have to get up to turn it off.

Some apps make it even harder to sleep in, by forcing you to engage in mentally stimulating activities like solving a puzzle to stop the beeping. "Do whatever works to keep you from hitting snooze,"

Chapter 10:

HOW TO DEVELOP AN INCREDIBLE WORK ETHIC

We've all been there. That feeling of really, really not wanting to go into the office of a morning. It cripples productivity, raises stress levels, and makes us unhappy.

Why Do We Do It To Ourselves?

Unless it stems from deeper issues, the feeling of not wanting to go to work is often the result of a poor work ethic. If you've experienced it yourself recently, that doesn't make you a bad person or employee. A poor work ethic usually arrives subconsciously and is something you'll have little control over or forewarning of its impending arrival.

Thankfully, there are some methods you can employ to improve your work ethic dramatically, and they're not quite as tricky as you might think. To help you get out of that rut and back, fighting fit for a productive time in the office, we've decided to list our top eight tips for improving your work ethic.

1. Start With Your Body – Treat It Right

A healthy body will help you build a healthy approach to work because the two are intrinsically linked.

If you feel lethargic in the morning, the last thing you're going to want to do is to spring out of bed and head to the office. You're far more likely to continually hit the 'snooze' button and curse the fact you even have a job.

Lethargy can be a result of not enough sleep and poor levels of exercise. Therefore if the feeling just described is something you're all too familiar with, it's time to go on something of a permanent health kick. And that doesn't mean ditching all the treats that make you happy – just the process of regularly exercising and eating more healthily.

Walk when you'd normally take the car and swap those regular naughty treats for fruit and glasses of water – you'll be surprised how much more up for it you'll feel each morning.

2. Eliminate As Many Distractions As Possible

How many times do you check your email each day? What about social media? Is your facebook feed something you access every five minutes to check in on what your friends and family are up to?

We live in a world full of distractions. Multiple forms of content, relentless notifications and devices capable of connecting us immediately to the internet are everywhere and seemingly impossible to drag yourself away from.

That's true – unless you can call on your reserves of willpower. Distractions will divert your attention from what matters, and ensure that you have a limited focus on work tasks. In turn, that'll reduce your emotional connection with the business and negatively impact your work ethic.

Check your email only two or three times a day, turn off notifications and leave social media for the moments when you're sat on the sofa with nothing better to do.

3. Measure Your Ethic Against Others

If you're forever cursing your colleague's ability to practically skip into work ready for the day ahead, why not measure your performance against theirs?

Something is different. It might be their mindset, attitude towards their role or lifestyle, but if you can be brave enough to measure your performance against others, you'll quickly suss out where you need to improve.

This can extend far beyond work colleagues, too. For example, if your partner appears to be having the time of their life at work, yet you can barely muster the strength to log onto your computer for the first time each morning, ask them how they're doing it. You never know – you might just learn a thing or two.

Unless you're particularly spritely in the morning, it's unlikely that you'll jump out of bed and head to work full of an endless supply of energy. Still, if you follow our tips above, you'll greatly increase your ability to foster a healthy approach to work. Whenever you feel uninspired by your role, but you know it's something more superficial than job dissatisfaction, check that you're doing all you can to improve your work ethic. As we've demonstrated today, it isn't that difficult at all.

Chapter 11:

6 Tricks To Become More Aware Of Your Strengths

"Strength and growth come only through continuous effort and struggle." - Napoleon Hill.

While it is true that we tend to focus more on our weaknesses than on our strengths, it is also true that we should polish our strengths more than our weaknesses. This in no way means that we should consider ourselves superior to others and start looking away from that we have flaws. Unfortunately, most of us don't spend much time on self-reflection and self-awareness. But they are the vital aspects if we are thinking of improving ourselves in any way.

Here are 6 Tricks to become more aware of your strengths:

1. Decide to be more self-aware

Human beings are complicated creatures. Our minds are designed so that we tend to absorb more negative than positive thoughts about ourselves and others. For this reason, self-awareness is perhaps the most crucial thing in an individual's life. Self-awareness is the ability to look deep inside of yourself and monitor your emotions and reactions. It is the ability to allow yourself to be aware of your strengths, weaknesses, as well as your triggers, motivators, and other characteristics. We'll help you find a set of tricks and techniques that you can apply to polish your strengths in a self-awareness way; and how to use your strengths in a promising way.

2. Meditation:

The first thought that will come to your mind would be, "Is this person crazy? How can meditation help us improve our strengths?" But hear me out. The fresh breeze of the morning when everything is at peace, and you sit there inhaling all the good energy in and the bad energy out, your mind and thoughts would automatically become slow-paced and calm. Once you get to relax with yourself, you can analyze the things that have been happening in your life and develop possible solutions on how you can deal with them using your strengths. The positive energy and calming mood you will get after meditating would help you make your decisions wisely when you are under pressure and your mind is in chaos.

3. Labelling your thoughts:

More often, our thoughts reflect on our behavior and what makes us fail or succeed in life. People can genuinely relate to a situation where they could have possibly thought about a worst-case scenario, but in the end, nothing as such happened. Our anxiety and hopelessness don't come from the situation we are struggling with, but rather our thoughts make us believe in the worst possible things that could happen to us. But we're stronger than we give ourselves credit for. We have the power to control our negative thoughts and turn them into positive ones. We can list all the ideas and thinking that provide us with stress and tension and then label them as either useful or useless. If the particular thought is causing a significant effect in your life, you can work towards it to make your life better and less anxious. Know your priorities and take help from your strengths to tackle the problems.

4. **Befriending your fears:**

There's not a single person on this planet who isn't afraid of something. Be it the fear of losing your loved ones or any phobias of either animal, insects, heights, closed spaces, etc. There are also so many fears related to our self-worth and whether we are good enough, skilled enough, or deserving enough of anything. To accept these fears and work towards overcoming them is perhaps the most powerful thing one could do. It takes so much of a person's strength and willpower to befriend fear, reduce it, and finally eliminate it. Most of the time, we end up in situations that we always feared, and then we have to take quick actions and make wise decisions. To remain calm in such cases and use your strengths and experiences to tackle whatever's in front of you is a remarkable quality found in only a few. But we can also achieve and polish this quality by strengthening our minds and preparing ourselves to get us out of situations wisely and effectively. To be patient and look into the problems from every angle is the critical component of this one.

5. **Watching your own movie:**

Narrating your life experiences to yourself or a close friend and telling yourself and them how far you have come can boost your self-confidence immensely. You should go in flashbacks and try to remember all the details of your life. You will find that there were some moments you felt immense joy and some moments where you felt like giving up. But with all the strength that you were collecting along the way, you endured the possible tortures and struggles and challenges and eventually rose again. So you should focus and be well aware of how you tackle those situations, what powers you have, and the strengths that couldn't let you give up but face everything. Once you have found the answers to the above questions, like for example, it was your patience and bravery that helped you through it, or it was your wise and speedy decisions that made it all effective, you can understand what strengths you have and make use of them later in life too.

6. Motivate yourself:

We should stop looking for others to notice how great we did or stop waiting for a round of applause or a pat on the back from them. Instead, we should motivate ourselves every time we fall apart, and we should have the energy to pick ourselves back up again. The feeling of satisfaction we get after completing a task or helping someone, that feeling is what we should strive for. We should become proud of ourselves and our strengths, as well as our weaknesses, that they helped us transform into the person we are today. We should never feel either superior or inferior to others. Everyone has their own pace and their own struggles. Our strengths should not only be for ourselves but for others too. Kindness, empathy, hospitality, being there for people, patience, courage, respect are all the qualities that one must turn into their strengths.

Conclusion:

The key to perfection is self-awareness. There's a fine line between who you are and who you strive to become; it can be achieved by becoming aware of your strengths, polishing them, and creating a sense of professional as well as personal development. Your strengths motivate you to try new things, achieve new skills, become a better version of yourself. Your strengths are what keeps you positive, motivated, help you to maintain your stress better, aid you in your intuitive decision making, and command you to help others as well. It inspires you to become a better person.

Chapter 12:

Happy People Don't Sweat the Small Stuff.

Stress follows a peculiar principle: when life hits us with big crises—the death of a loved one or a job loss—we somehow find the inner strength to endure these upheavals in due course. It's the little things that drive us insane day after day—traffic congestion, awful service at a restaurant, an overbearing coworker taking credit for your work, meddling in-laws, for example.

It's all too easy to get caught up in the many irritations of life. We overdramatize and overreact to life's myriad tribulations. Under the direct influence of anguish, our minds are bewildered, and we feel disoriented. This creates stress, which makes the problems more difficult to deal with.

The central thesis of psychotherapist Richard Carlson's bestselling ***Doesn't Sweat The Small Stuff... And It's All Small Stuff*** (1997) is this: to deal with angst or anger, we need not some upbeat self-help prescriptions for changing ourselves, but simply a measure of perspective.

Perspective helps us understand that there's an art to understand what we should let go of and what we should concern ourselves with. It is important to focus our efforts on the important stuff and not waste time on insignificant and incidental things.

I've previously written about my favorite 5-5-5 technique for gaining perspective and guarding myself against anger erupting: I remove myself from the offending environment and contemplate if whatever I'm getting worked up over is of importance. I ask myself, "Will this matter in 5 days? Will this matter in 5 months? Will this matter in 5 years?"

Carlson stresses that there's always a vantage point from which even the biggest stressor can be effectively dealt with. The challenge is to keep making that shift in perspective. When we achieve that "wise-person-in-me" perspective, our problems seem more controllable and our lives more peaceful.

Carlson's prescriptions aren't uncommon—we can learn to be more patient, compassionate, generous, grateful, and kind, all of which will improve the way we feel about ourselves and how other people feel when they are around us.

Some of Carlson's 100 recommendations are trite and banal—for example, "make peace with imperfection," "think of your problems as potential teachers," "remember that when you die, your 'in-basket' won't be empty," and "do one thing at a time." Others are more informative:

- Let others have the glory

- Let others be "right" most of the time

- Become aware of your moods, and don't allow yourself to be fooled by the low ones

- Look beyond behavior

- Every day, tell at least one person something you like, admire, or appreciate about them.

- Argue for your limitations, and they're yours

- Resist the urge to criticize

- Read articles and books with entirely different points of view from your own and try to learn something.

Chapter 13:

A Guided Journal For Anxiety

Anxiety is the silent killer.

Anxiety is a state of worry when you are unsure about the next step. Very few people know how to handle anxiety when they face it. Instead, they bury their heads in the sand and hope that things will eventually work themselves out.

What remains unclear are the disastrous results of actions resulting from anxiety. Healthy relationships have collapsed when partners succumbed to anxiety, job opportunities have been lost, and once-in-a-lifetime chances have slipped from our hands because we were unable to contain the anxiety that was building in us.

We will lose count of the much that anxiety has cost us. Sometimes, it has been misconstrued as a "normal" feeling and nothing is done to tame it. That is the moment the rain starts beating us. Nothing much can be done when we realize the damage anxiety has done in our lives.

Here is a guided journal for anxiety:

i.   Take a step back.

Sometimes we are anxious because we do not understand what we are into. We get nervous about new experiences and do not know how to proceed from there. Our judgment is often clouded when we are in unfamiliar territories. The fear of not being right builds anxiety in us and we want to please everybody. What a herculean task!

Take a step back to get the bigger picture. This will bring clarity because you can look at all variables at once and weigh them, one after another. Moving back gives you a sense of power and control when you realize it was not that difficult in the first place. You will be more comfortable in an environment you can manipulate.

Anxiety results from the fear of the unknown. When you withdraw a little from a situation, you can comfortably evaluate it because nobody will judge you.

   ii.   <u>Take off your mind from the subject matter.</u>

This is an evasion strategy. You are not always required to face your fears immediately. It is okay to withdraw your attention when you are anxious about something or an unprecedented condition. You will live to tackle it another day. Do not pressure yourself to act within a deadline. The timeframes you confine yourself within will haunt you especially when you feel inadequate for what is ahead of you.

Put your mind on things that bring you solace and calm to fight the anxiety. You understand yourself better than anyone does and you are best placed to make this decision. Think about your dream car – Rolls-Royce, Ferrari, Porsche, Chevrolet, or any other that fascinates you. Relaxing thoughts will calm you down and kick away anxiety.

Our comfort zones give us confidence because we can handle ourselves better in them. Anxiety cannot win the battle when we are in them.

iii.   <u>Do not think of any consequences – there are none.</u>

There are no consequences of acting right. What gives anxiety room to thrive is the fear of consequences that will befall us if we do not act expectedly. Deny anxiety the pleasure of tormenting you by not accepting liability for doing the right thing.

Even in situations that present a dilemma, choose to do the right thing over the popular choice. Populism is not always right and its consequences are unavoidable. They will finally come to haunt you. To be safe, make the right choice whose consequences are positive and will bring you honor.

Regardless of how quickly you will want to work on your anxiety and make a popular choice, its results are indelible. Purpose to cure anxiety through the right channel with positive consequences.

iv.   <u>Consult widely.</u>

Consultations are the preserve of the wise. Only the wise accept that they do not have a monopoly of ideas. They seek the opinions of other people who could have had a similar experience. When you find yourself in a compromising situation, remember that you are not the first person to experience the same. Someone else has been there and they made it.

Anxiety grows in ignorance. You get nervous because you do not know how to handle the challenge your way. Seek the advice of experienced people and they will guide you on how to navigate unchartered territories.

In conclusion, anyone could be anxious. What makes the difference is how different people handle it. Some turn it into an opportunity for growth while others allow it to kill their dreams. Make the right choice.

Chapter 14:

HOW TO AVOID BURNOUT

Stress may be unavoidable, but burnout is preventable. Following these steps may help you thwart stress from getting the best of you:

Exercise

Not only is exercise good for our physical health, but it can also give us an emotional boost.

Stretched for time? You don't need to spend hours at the gym to reap these benefits. Mini-workouts and short walks are convenient ways to make exercise a daily habit.

Eat A Balanced Diet

Eating a healthy diet filled with omega-3 fatty acids can be a natural antidepressant. Adding foods rich in omega-3s like flaxseed oil, walnuts, and fish may help give your mood a boost.

Practice Good Sleep Habits

Our bodies need time to rest and reset, which is why healthy sleep habits are essential for our well-being.

Avoiding caffeine before bedtime, establishing a relaxing bedtime ritual, and banning smartphones from the bedroom can help promote sound sleep hygiene.

Ask For Help

During stressful times, it's important to reach out for help. If asking for assistance feels difficult, consider developing a self-ca6re "check-in" with close friends and family members so that you can take care of each other during trying times.

How To Help Friends Or Family Members

How can you help someone experiencing burnout? While you can't take away someone's stress, offering support can help lighten their emotional load.

Listen

Before jumping into "fixing" mode, offer to listen to your friend or family member's difficulties.

Having someone to talk to can make a world of difference. Often people need someone to witness their stress and suffering, and listening can go a long way.

Validate Feelings And Concerns

When friends and family members are feeling the effects of burnout, saying *it doesn't sound that bad* or *i'm sure things will get better* — while meant to offer reassurance — can feel invalidating if someone is feeling low and hopeless.

Instead, offer validation by saying, "you've been working so hard, i can understand why you feel depleted."

Offer Specific Types Of Help

Individuals who are burnt out are often too tired to think of ways that others can help them. Instead of asking, "how can i help?" Offer to drop off a meal, pick up dry cleaning, or do a load of laundry.

Kind Gestures

Sending flowers, a thoughtful text message, or a written card can remind friends and family members that they're not alone.

Because they're often working long hours, people with burnout can feel lonely and underappreciated. But small gestures of kindness can be nurturing.

Research Resources

If friends or family members need additional support, like childcare, a house cleaner, or a psychotherapist, offer to research and crowdsource for specific resources to help ease the stress.

Being exposed to continual stress can cause us to burnout. Feelings of exhaustion, anxiety, and isolating from friends and family members can be some of the signs. However, eating a balanced diet, regular exercise, and getting a good night's sleep may prevent this stressed state.

Worried about friends and family members who may be burnt out? Listening to their concerns, validating their emotions, and offering specific types of support can help lighten the load.

Burnout can be avoided by making self-care part of your daily routine. Even if you're working long hours, studying for exams, or taking care of young children, remember to sprinkle some joy into each day.

Try going for a walk, talking to a friend, or watching an enjoyable program on television. Small self-care gestures like these can stop stress from turning into something more serious, like burnout.

Chapter 15:

7 Ways Your Behaviors Are Holding You Back

Habits and behaviors are what defines a human being and make you who you are. It is what shapes us and defines our lives while making us move towards our future. However, did you know that there are multiple things that hold you back?

These are the behavior that molds us, defines us, holds us back to be the better person and achieves everything that it takes to be perfect. Well, not that anyone is perfect; however, we all can aspire to be! Isn't it so? Let us explore and discuss the ways that your behaviors hold you back.

1. Not Accepting Your Faults

We have all been guilty of doing the same. Haven't we? I am so sure that each one of you has at least once committed this sin of shifting the blame to someone else and removing it off your shoulders. We are humans, after all; we are governed by our hearts, more than our minds. This is why we are more inclined to never accepting our faults instead of putting the blame on others.

Irrespective of the circumstance, it is necessary that you accept your fault, realize your weakness, and evaluate what needs to be done in order to never repeat the same. Going forward, you must find a way to turn your weakness into strength.

2. Having Self-Doubt

A lot of us are seen killing our dreams due to fear of being rejected. Haven't you already done the same a few times? Well, we all have! Self-doubt is one of the silent killers that can do you more harm than any good. If you constantly find yourself doubting your potential and stuck in a negative situation, you need to know that you are holding yourself back.

You can only look forward and attain a prosperous tomorrow when you stop doubting yourself. Self-doubt can be highly injurious, and this is one big reason why you need to stop holding yourself back and take a giant leap forward, or maybe a baby step! Shall we?

3. Procrastinating On Everything

No matter how many times we decide not to keep doing it, we keep doing it! Let's face it, and there are way too many distractions for us to procrastinate and sideline our current goals and duties. Say hello to social media! It distracts you way too many times than it should, especially when you are on the verge of serving your last-minute deadlines!

Hasn't it already got way too annoying? If it has, you must take a deep breath and train your mind. This is one of the behaviors that might hold you back. When you find yourself in such a situation, you must stop procrastinating; instead, do what you are supposed to do. Doing this will help you largely concentrate and uplift productivity.

4. Disrespecting Others

Do you often find yourself engaging in putting others down? If yes, then let me tell you that you are only inviting a lot of ill wrath for yourself. Imagine telling yourself that you are incapable, you are not good enough, and stuffs similar.

Similarly, if you do the same things to others, you are dragging everyone down. This is why you must stop being the harsh person that you are being and put your negativity aside. Disrespecting others or putting others down will only do more harm to you and your mental well-being. Why not focus more on what you can do to uplift others, encourage others and bring in more positivity around yourself!

5. Being In Your Cozy Corner

Not literally, but what we mean is you being in your own comfort zone! We all need our own comfort zones to feel safe and secured! But did you know that this is one such habit that holds you back? Yes, it holds you back from achieving a lot many things that you have only dreamt of. When you stay in your own comfort zone, you will never know what you are capable of.

Hence, unless and until you try your hands on something and step out of your comfort zone, you will never know what you are truly capable of. Did you know that the brawny in the business, such as Bill Gates, Warren Buffet, and many other personalities, have all failed in life, at some point or the other! But what would have happened if they would have feared their failure and stayed in their comfort zone for the rest of their lives?

Remember, with the risk comes to the possibility of achieving a reward. Hence, why hold yourself back and stay in your comfort zone when you can explore, wander and try everything that comes your way to know what you are capable of! Imagine what a great learning experience it will be!

6. Waiting For The Right Moment

Do you really think that there is a right moment for everything? If there were, then the law of gravity would not have been discovered, neither would we have received more significant innovations in life. Well, it is up to you to choose a moment and act! Yes, it is as simple as that!

If you keep living your life wandering about the right moment that will control your life and that you have your own sweet time to do everything, you will only lose on your precious time. Instead, we all must be accountable for our actions each day and grab the opportunity to try, create, explore, invent, experiment, and a lot more!

7. The Image of Being Perfect

Don't we feel that everyone around us is living their perfect lives? Sorry to burst your bubble, it is not so! Thanks to social media, we are always misguided to believe that others live their fairytales while we are sulking in our own lives! This is when we keep pushing ourselves to live a perfect life, be a perfect person and make everyone around us perfect!

But is it practically possible to do so? In fact, with doing so, we tend to set an unrealistic expectation and tends to harm our mental well being and relationships around us. Life is about swinging in the right direction at times, and sometimes in the opposite! Each of these scenarios brings with it its fruits, which must be graced with positivity.

Hence, let me tell you, there is no need for you to be perfect! Be however you are, but be your best version!

Conclusion:

Hence, kill these behaviors that hold you back. Instead, break the barrier and strive for a rewarding tomorrow. Let's try being a little different than we are? What say?

Chapter 16:

10 Habits That Will Make Your Life Better

All of us desire to have better lives. We hope that someday we will have progressive and substantive lives. We should be alive to the fact that a dream without concrete plans to realize it will remain just that – a dream on paper. Our habits cumulatively bring us closer to a better life. Here are ten habits that will make your life better:

1. Honesty

Success is founded on honest work. Honesty is the backbone of a better life. To succeed, you have to be honest with yourself and other people. Doing honest work and relating with people truthfully will establish you as reliable.

Honesty is rare and when people perceive you are reliable, they will entrust you with their resources and other factors of production

2. Continuously Learning New Things

We are in a constant state of learning. It is a continuous endless process that helps us become better daily. Even the most educated people have a new life concept to learn from other people. In learning, we unlearn myths, fallacies, and misconceptions. You can improve your life by learning a new skill that will aid you to face new challenges in life. Not everything is learned in a classroom, some lessons are acquired through experience. Purpose to learn throughout your life and your life will improve.

3. Accepting Correction

Nobody is perfect. Everybody has their flaws and the earlier you identify your weaknesses and work on them, the better things will get for you. Correction does not mean that you are incompetent but rather imperfect like everybody else.

Own up to your mistakes and do not be defensive when you are corrected. The first step towards improvement is accepting your wrongs and implementing the right suggestions.

4. Boldness To Make Tough Decisions

Sometimes you need to make landmark decisions in your life. It could be severing close ties with some people or being ruthless in abandoning old retrogressive habits. A better life is guaranteed if you make the right decisions. Fortune favors the bold. Better opportunities will come when you venture into new business spaces. Although the hesitancy in trying new things is real, evaluate the possible value arising from the bold step you will take.

5. Good Socializing Habits

Making friends fast is an important life skill. It is beneficial for you to easily blend in a given setting and make friends with strangers. When you are in a new space, get to know people because they can help you navigate unfamiliar territories. Good socializing habits will protect you from attacks when new people you meet profile you as unfriendly.

6. Quick Adaptability To The Environment

Do not seek preferential treatment whenever you are in a new environment. Adapt to the prevailing conditions and you will blend well with the local population.Moreover, you can focus on other important issues when you spend little time settling down. Quick adaptability will make you live peacefully wherever life takes you.

7. Creativity

Creativity can hardly be learned formally. It is mostly acquired through experience and personal zeal. Life is a cycle with many unique challenges. You cannot tackle every challenge in the same way.
Creativity will help you come up with new ways of approaching issues. Things will work out for you when you think out of the ordinary.

8. Building Bridges

It is important not to create enmity everywhere you go because you could be unknowingly shutting doors to future opportunities. Build bridges and not walls with people you meet because the future is uncertain. Life would be easier when you do not have many enemies to worry about. Your focus would be on more important matters.

9. Consulting

Nobody has a monopoly on ideas. Seeking advice is not a sign of weakness but an appreciation that you do not know everything. You have nothing to lose and instead stand to gain a lot from the advice you get. Instead of acting blindly, consult experienced people on issues you are naïve at. Consultation is an eye-opener to many things. You can thereafter make sober decisions.

10. Complying With Authority

Every place has rules that govern the place. Law brings order and streamlines issues where there is no clarity. Seek to fulfill what is required of you wherever you are by the existing authority. It is responsible for the creation of a conducive working environment. When you comply with set rules, you contribute to your success and that of others.

In conclusion, these ten habits will make your life better. They are the existing habits of successful people. We can be like them when we follow in their steps.

Chapter 17:

Overcome Demotivation

Human life is very short and keeps getting shorter and shorter with each day. In this short life we feel discouraged and every other moment or every other day. We get frustrated and we tend to lose hope.

But then good days come too and we feel on top of the world. Our hearts are overfilled with joy and satisfaction but this too lasts for some time and then life surprises us with some new big rock of grief or depression. This moment though short can take us down a deep hole where we don't see a way back up.

This is the moment of everyone's life where they are the most demotivated to do anything in life. No matter how much our loved ones try to get us to try one more time, we keep sinking deeper into self-rejection and denial.

This feeling of not being motivated no matter what good comes around time after time is not helpful for anyone even if you need to become the world's most successful person.

But there are countless things you can do to deviate your mind from any such situation. Let's discuss some.

I'll say, you get up right away, tighten up some shoes and get out on a long run. Try to look around you and find anyone else who can apparently be in any distress. Approach them if you can and help them in any way possible if they allow you to.

Try to feel others' pain and surely you will be thankful for what you already have in life.
If you don't feel like going out that's OK too; pick up the phone and call anyone who you think might care for the most for what you are going through right now. If you have someone who can relate to you in such times of greys and blacks, you surely have an escape route.

You might think you are sitting alone on your couch in your sweats and wandering over random things to take your mind off.

But the reality is that every now and then in such alone moments you wander off in conditions where you somehow end up comparing yourself with someone else and rather than being inspired by that person, you feel jealous and might curse someone. You start to think what they have is perfect and you can never be there. But the reality is they are there because they knew how to overcome these feelings you have right now.

So reorder yourself. Make a new plan. Make a new scheme for what you should be doing when the next fire breaks in your life. What you can do to overcome the next rejection.

Things have always a way to release you. Events can leave an impact but that impact doesn't necessarily have to stamp rather a lesson to take new paths. You don't want to put your hands in the same hole again where you were once bitten. You just need to find a way to get around the hole and keep the track you were once on!

Chapter 18:

Six Triggers That Make New Habits Stick

Character development does not stop at developing new habits. It also includes making them stick to form your personality. Overhauling a person's personality is not a walk in the park. This explains why many people are unable to stick to their New Year resolutions of adopting new desirable habits.

You may shift the blame of your failure of permanently adopting new progressive habits from one reason to another. To succeed, it has to be a self-initiative to make things work for you.

These six triggers make new habits stick:

1. Change Your Company

Bad company ruins good morals. This life lesson is true even when people try to convince themselves otherwise. Your circle of friends determines your behavior. They are powerful to turn your personality inside out. The habits of the company you keep will most likely infect you and before you know it, you will start behaving like them.

When you have decided to adopt new habits contrary to those of your friends, you will fail if you retain their company. You have to dissociate with them for the new habits you adopt to stick. In their place, find like-minded friends with whom you share a common purpose.

2. Practice Persistently

You should regularly practice the new habit you desire to adopt for it to stick. Practice makes perfect. You become used to a new habit if it forms part of your routine. With time, the habit no longer becomes tedious but enjoyable. You get to embrace it more and before you know it, it has found its place in your lifestyle.

If you want to develop a reading habit, ensure you read some literature daily. Intentionally select the genre of literature that thrills you and read continuously not just when it is convenient. The effort and practice you put towards this will make the reading habit stick permanently.

3. Set Alarms and Reminders

Alarms and reminders are a constant signal calling you out to attend to something you had dedicated time to do. We set alarms, reminders, or both to make us remember our dedication to doing a task we intended. They are vital to holding us accountable for a decision we made.

Omnipresence is a trait human beings lack. Reminders do the due diligence of not letting you forget to do something you intended and scheduled time for. When you set alarms to remind you to do something, you will always remember it. With time, an alarm becomes unnecessary because the new habit would have stuck and formed your routine.

4. Learn More About The New Habit

Knowledge is power. When you seek knowledge on a new habit that you intend to adopt and make it stick, you understand how easy or difficult your journey shall be. This makes you prepared for any eventuality. When you face difficulty when things get tough, it does not come as a surprise and you will soldier on to continue with your new habit.

Your insight into the new habits you want to make stick is important because it will inform how you relate with your family and friends. Moreover, you get to be more effective in adopting these habits unlike when an ignorant person tries adopting the same.

5. Be Disciplined

Discipline is the glue that guarantees your commitment. The lack of it seals your failure towards any cause you set your heart to. When you are undisciplined, you will overlook many things that contribute to your success in making a habit stick. Introducing a foreign habit into your lifestyle is a tedious task if you lack the discipline to keep you going.

Indiscipline is responsible for many failed missions. You have to be a disciplined person to succeed in anything. It cannot apply selectively. When you pass the discipline test, the new habits you adopt shall stick. To aid you to have discipline, penalize yourself whenever you fail in something. Consequences will enable you to adopt new habits successfully.

6. Be Self-Driven

Habits that sprout from within are more likely to stick compared to those instilled in us by authorities. People adhere to the latter more than they do to the former. It is paramount that the drive to adopt a new habit be a self-driven initiative because you will follow it.

There is rebellion and resistance if people take on certain habits by force or if they do out of fear of the possible ramifications that they might face. You have to first love a habit and purpose to practice it for you to be successful in making it stick in your lifestyle.

In conclusion, these six triggers will make new habits stick only if you apply them correctly.

Chapter 19:

How To Do A Life Audit To Get Your Life Together

'New year, new me' - at least that's what most of us are thinking come January. It's the most common time of the year to want to make a change and sort your life out. But only 8% of us will keep to our New Year's resolutions, while the rest will struggle because we've either set too many, they are unrealistic - or we lose motivation entirely, get fed up, and drop all interest in it! So if you often find yourself asking, 'how can I change my life?' come to New Year, we suggest you try doing a Life Audit, which helps you take charge, assessing what you want and how to go and get it. It's a great way to learn how to improve your life for the better. Here's how...

1. START WITH POST-IT NOTES
Write everything down that you want to achieve, your goals, hopes, and dreams.

2. CATEGORIZE WHAT'S IMPORTANT
Group your Post-its into the areas that you want to work on. This could be health, finances, relationships, work, or exercise.

3. DO A NOW-OR-NEVER AUDIT

Once you've written down all your goals, stick them in a clear, visible place. Take a good look at each goal. Go through each one and ask yourself two questions, 'Is this important?' and 'Is this what I want?' If the answer is no and you think you'd be happy if you didn't do it, then get rid of it.

4. ASK SOME BIG QUESTIONS

Draw a circle, divide it into eight sections. Give each segment a part of your life, like relationships or fitness. This is where you ask yourself the important stuff! Which areas should you give more focus to, which bits need more work, and more importantly, which areas give your life meaning?

5. CLOSE THE GAP

Time to get practical! Choose realistic steps to bridge the gap between now and where you want to be. But remember - be realistic with yourself!

6. CREATE A TIMELINE

Decide what to do first and when you'd like to do it. You don't need to make big changes; many smaller steps can lead to a bigger and better change.

7. ENLIST SUPPORT

Friends and family are there for a reason. Let them know what you're doing, but choose carefully. You want someone who will support and won't question what you're doing and help you improve your life. The final step in a good life audit is summarizing your insights.

To do this, look for common themes and write out a clear picture of your life as it currently is. Having this life audit summary will help you decide what is adding value to your life, what you can let go of, and what actions you need to take.

Chapter 20:

Stop Thinking and Start Doing

What is going on around you right now? I am not asking this rather telling you because I know most of you are already thinking the same question. You should be asking this question, or should you?

We are a two-faced species. We say something upfront but we adopt the opposite for ourselves at the same time. We want to install a certain methodology in everyone around us but we are ashamed to do the same thing ourselves.

Fear is a more appropriate and less offending word some might say. But why is it? Is something harmful, or something that doesn't make sense only when you yourself are in the same place as others that followed you?

So show off when we don't have something good to contribute in our own lives? Why be a hypocrite who doesn't even have the guts to admit that they are the timidest and lucid person and they want to follow their own instincts?

You have to make those small changes in your life. That will one day result in a bigger change and elevate your life to that ultimate stature, then you are probably dead.

Stop preaching, stop playing around, stop thinking, worrying, wondering, doubting fearing, hoping for some easy way out! Learn to say STOP to everything that goes against your instincts and your wishes for a better tomorrow.

Do you think you are grinding away yourself every day so you deserve a break? No!

What makes you think you have achieved all you can?

Sure you have done a lot in your life, sometimes it was due to circumstances, sometimes your talents, and sometimes just pure luck. But you went through it then and you were very less competent back then! So why can't you do some more things like those, just easier?

You can and you will! Because now you have grown within and have more experience to tackle what needs to be tackled.

If you keep telling yourself and keep thinking, "Oh this wasn't meant to happen", or "Was it my fault?", or "Why does it always have to be me?", you will quite look over your shoulder searching for the easy way out!

Learn to live by the chances that you keep getting every day. Because is too short to be wondering and never to lift a finger and point in the direction of what needs to be done.

Don't act like you are totally blank and have no idea what to do next. Take a moment and your instincts will naturally take you to the best possible solution.

But you have to get up, go out and start pursuing. Because you are your first priority, always was and always should be.

There is a time in everyone's life when they just need to stop thinking and start doing. That time is always the previous second. The day you understand this puzzle, give yourself a tap on the shoulder because you have finally outgrown yourself

Chapter 21:

Happy People Are Proactive About Relationships

Researchers have found that as human beings we are only capable of maintaining up to 150 meaningful relationships, including five primary, close relationships.

This holds true even with the illusion of thousands of "friends" on social media platforms such as Facebook, Instagram, and Twitter. If you think carefully about your real interactions with people, you'll find the five close/150 extended relationships rule holds true.

Perhaps not coincidentally, Tony Robbins, the personal development expert, and others argue that your attitudes, behavior, and success in life are the sum total of your five closest relationships. So, toxic relationships, toxic life.

With this in mind, it's essential to continue to develop relationships that are positive and beneficial. **But in today's distracted world, these relationships won't just happen.**

We need to be proactive about developing our relationships.

My current favorite book on personal development is Tim Ferriss's excellent, though long, 700+ page book, *Tools of Titans: The Tactics, Routines, and Habits of Billionaires, Icons, and World-Class Performers.*

At one point, Ferriss quotes retired women's volleyball great Gabby Reece:

I always say that I'll go first.... That means if I'm checking out at the store, I'll say "hello" first. If I'm coming across somebody and make eye contact, I'll smile first. [I wish] people would experiment with that in their life a little bit: be first, because — not all times, but most times — it comes in your favor... The response is pretty amazing.... I was at the park the other day with the kids.

Oh, my God. Hurricane Harbor [water park]. It's like hell. There were these two women a little bit older than me. We couldn't be more different, right? And I walked by them, and I just looked at them and smiled. The smile came to their face so instantly. They're ready, but you have to go first because now we're being trained in this world [to opt out] — nobody's going first anymore.

Be proactive: start the conversation

I agree. I was excited to read this principle because I adopted this by default years ago, and it's given me the opportunity to hear the most amazing stories and develop the greatest relationships you can imagine.

On airplanes, in the grocery store, at lunch, I've started conversations that led to trading heartfelt stories, becoming friends, or doing business together. A relationship has to start someplace, and that can be any place in any moment.

Be proactive: lose your fear of being rejected

I also love this idea because it will help overcome one of the main issues I hear from my training and coaching clients – the fear of making an initial connection with someone they don't know.

This fear runs deep for many people and may be hardwired in humans. We are always observing strangers to determine if we can trust them – whether they have positive or dangerous intent.

In addition, **we fear rejection. Our usual negative self-talk says something like,** *If I start the conversation, if I make eye contact, if I smile, what if it's not returned?*

What if I'm rejected, embarrassed, or ignored by no response? I'll feel like an idiot, a needy loser.

Chapter 22:

Building Confidence

The things we strive for all our lives are a mere image of what we can achieve and what we want to achieve.

There is a difference between two very important aspects of our life. One is self-esteem and the other is self-confidence. You have very high self-esteem if you think big of yourself and have respect for your craft. This is a very important thing to have because no one is big on confidence if they don't have a good opinion about themselves.

We often say that 'You and You only are your best critic'. This isn't a statement for the narrow-minded.

If you think big of yourself, you will have a better perspective of the things you do and wish to do someday. If you have a 'No Go' confidence towards everything, then you have nothing to start with.

Do you want to build confidence? Take some tips, just as a piece of advice.

If you want to build confidence, Focus on what you can't do, not on what you can't. I know this is against everything we think someone will say to boost your morale.

But the truth is, that when you start to work on things that you cannot do, you will try it for some time, but then you will eventually fail. That might prove to be a breaking point for some people.

If you focus on what you can do, you will always be successful. And you will praise your good work, and that will help you every time exponentially. The more you proceed, the more you will succeed and the more you will be confident in yourself.

You also need to surround yourself with people who believe in you.

Every person in his life has had a moment when they were just about to summit the biggest achievement of their life. But gave up or lost hope because they let the noise and opinions around them get into their heads.

Those who have opinions have nothing else going on in their lives. So they try to mend their souls by inflicting negation on others. You don't have time or energy to deal with these people.

So keep the people in your life who have the same approach towards life as you and they love you for who you are. These people will help you in even the darkest deepest days of your life.

The last piece of advice is what we have heard from the first step that we took in our childhood. The advice of never giving up!

You will fail here and there everywhere in your life. You are meant to fail. Everyone is meant to fail someday. But you cannot give up! You Should Never Give Up!

We have a lot of things going on in our lives and one or the other is meant to fall apart someday. We lose money. We lose friends. We lose family. But what you cannot lose forever is Hope.

Till the day you have hope, you have a reserve to keep you on the track and maybe someday, fly like a phoenix.

Chapter 23:

Dealing with Difficult Bosses.

Sometimes bosses can be A bit difficult to handle because of their expectations and behavior with the employees. But they are not impossible to deal with. You should never be discouraged by their behavior. Some people resign because of this, but in the end, the boss is not the one who is affected by this bold step, but the employee who takes this decision is affected because finding A rewarding job is never easy. There are ways to deal with difficult bosses, and by doing so, an employee can achieve big things and, at the same time, learn how to work in this environment.

The first and foremost thing to do is to evaluate the aspect because of which the boss is being difficult to work for. After that, think of the stuff that can be done to tackle that aspect. Even difficult bosses are good when you give them good results. They can be very rewarding because their expectations are always very high, so if an employee performs according to their expectations, they reward that employee generously. Some bosses get annoyed when employees skip the office or are late for work. Even in situations like illness, they are reluctant to give days off. If your boss is like this, the only thing to do is reduce your chances of illness. If A boss is target-oriented, you should be very focused on your task and should try to complete it before time to eliminate any chance of trouble. The next solution is not to be associated with groups that always cause trouble for the organization. Bosses can give A very tough time to employees who delay the targets by causing unwanted trouble.

To get the boss' attention, you should be on good terms with the managers because they are the ones who report to the leader, so by being on good terms with the managers, they will speak highly of you with the boss, and he will be happy by our attitude which can reduce the chances of behavioral problems by the boss. Increasing productivity is the key to being in the good books of A boss. In the end, it all comes to profitability which leaders care about the most. So if you are A good asset to the organization, the boss will hardly ever bother you. Also, when in direct communication with the boss, an employee should be in A very presentable manner, not only in terms of clothing but also in terms of body language and presentation skills. Words should be chosen very carefully in front of bosses. Having good communication and presenting skills is the key to getting the boss' attention in A positive way.

Some bosses are indeed difficult to work for, but by following some basic rules of thumb, employees can work without the worry of the boss being annoyed. The key is to anticipate what the leader wants from his employees, and then it comes to meeting their expectations. Employees that prove to be A valuable asset for the organization are always rewarded by the leader because such employees are the reason for the organization's success. A company can be successful only if the boss and employees are willing to work together. Even if the boss is getting on your nerves, try not to let it get to you. Recognize your importance and work hard for your own sake.

Chapter 24:

6 Habits of Oprah Winfrey

When anyone utters the name "Oprah Winfrey," one of her most iconic quotes comes to mind: "You get a car, and everyone else gets a car." While most business people applaud the "to-do roster," Oprah is not one of them; instead, she values meditation, no alarms, and limiting business operations to the necessary minimum. From a poor rural Mississippi upbringing to getting a full scholarship and to landing a seat on the morning talk program, Baltimore Is Talking, to now solidifying her reputation as a global legend and America's first black billionaire, with a net worth of US$2.5 billion, you might be wondering – exactly how she does it?

Oprah Winfrey maintains a series of daily routines-from getting up early to work out to practicing Gratitude. This daily routine, as she notes, keeps her happy, grounded, and humble.

Here are six daily habits from the legend herself that you might want to make your own.

1. Her Day Starts With Morning Rituals

Oprah Winfrey starts her mornings with a sequence of spiritual exercises, allowing her body to wake up and her mind to focus on Gratitude and self-reflection. She meditates for approximately 20 minutes. If the weather is nice, she sits in her lawn chair with her eyes closed, simply reminiscing on the previous day and imagining her aspirations for the day ahead. She noted that starting the day slowly allows her mind to wake up and become entirely focused on the day ahead.

2. Working Out Every Morning

Oprah's journey to weight loss has been a struggle over the years. She opened up on her efforts with maintaining a healthy weight and fitness program. She highlighted in an interview that she loves sweating it up through the regular old-fashioned cardio exercises, explicitly on an elliptical machine followed by a treadmill. She then follows with some regular bodyweight training before warming up for some sit-ups.

Although there is ongoing research on whether a better fitness routine should be in the morning or the evening, substantial studies describe several morning fitness benefits. To mention a few, You'll eat fewer calories; you'll have more energy throughout the day, burn more bothersome fat cells, and sleep better when the sun goes down.

3. She Consumes a Lot of Vegetables

If you don't pay attention when your mother or your partner softly encourages you to eat more of Mother Earth's natural creations, maybe you'll listen to Oprah Winfrey.

Oprah confessed in an interview that she values her lunch more than any other meal, and one of her meals go-to involves a big, overflowing salad of green goodness. She noted that the salad is usually from the veggies from her home garden. As she put its's "as a rule, if we can grow it, we don't buy it."

You probably don't need us to tell you that veggies are excellent for your diet. Still, science backs up Winfrey's meal plan, as a well-balanced, vegetable patch diet can help fight cancer, heart disease, diabetes, and hypertension, among other conditions.

4. Oprah Schedules Time To Unwind

There's no doubt that Winfrey's itinerary would be overwhelming for most people, with regular meetings, phone conversations, and traveling, but achieving this degree of esteem necessitates astute management and perseverance. However, if you look into the lives of individuals at the pinnacle of success, such as Winfrey, you'll notice that they constantly make time to unwind.

In an interview about her daily life, Winfrey stated that she relaxes before retiring to bed by reading frequently. Though you may not have Winfrey's gorgeous fireplace to warm you up as you flip the pages over, the research found that individuals who read before bed are less anxious than those who watch Netflix.

5. Practicing Gratitude daily

The benefits of practicing Gratitude have been proven for centuries, even though gestures to the same have become popular recently. Oprah maintains with her volumes of gratitude diaries that she usually jots down before going to bed. She makes a list of things that have given her tremendous joy or which she is grateful for.

Implementing this habit will not only improve your health but also increase your empathy and self-confidence. One study suggests that thinking about what you're thankful for rather than contemplating on the to-do list each night helps better your sleep.

6. She Manages Her Finances

You'd think someone of Winfrey's caliber would employ someone to manage her finances, but while she got a whole team, she oversees the minutiae of her fortune daily. She claims that she cannot delegate all financial decisions to others because she had a poor upbringing and prefers to understand what comes in and what goes out of her earnings. She noted during an interview that it is crucial for her to personally manage her finances as doing so relieves her from surprises of what she has and doesn't have.

While most of us struggle with the very thought about money, research has shown that the more you train yourself to handle your finances, the better your chances of becoming wealthy.

Conclusion

Just as Oprah, if you are invariably striving to achieve greatness in all life aspects, you must maintain a couple of healthy habits. If Oprah's journey inspires you, then flexing to the above routine might be your thing. Who knows!

Chapter 25:

10 Habits For Good Health

Good health is great wealth that we can be proud of. It cannot be equated with any amount of possessions. We follow the doctors' instructions to the latter when we fall sick because we want to regain back our good health. Here are ten habits for good health:

1. Eating A Balanced Diet

A balanced diet is one of the basic principles of proper nutrition. It is a simple yet essential pillar in building good health. A balanced meal should contain all the required nutrients – carbohydrates, proteins, vitamins, and water –in correct proportions.

Taking a balanced diet requires discipline. Regardless of how much you love one type of food, you cannot eat it alone at the expense of other meals. Diversified meals with different nutritional values are important to the body.

2. Eating Fresh Food Only.

Fresh food is that which is not stale. It is important to take fresh food because they are not contaminated with bacteria that accumulate over time due to poor storage. Stale food introduces bacteria to our bodies that will make us fall sick.

Poorly preserved food poses a risk to our health. Hotels and restaurants adhere to guidelines of proper food handling to prevent food poisoning to their customers. Taking fresh food reduces the risk of falling sick.

3. Drinking Plenty Of Water.

The body majorly consists of water. It is an important part of a balanced diet. Water helps us hydrate and stay fit. So important is water that our bodies require it more than it does food.

It is recommended to take eight glasses of water in a day for us to stay hydrated because it is excreted in large quantities and we need to replenish it. Taking plenty of water also helps improve our skin tone.

4. Doing Physical Exercise.

Physical exercise is very important but often overlooked. Our bodies need exercise to stay fit and keep off lifestyle diseases. Exercises are also a form of therapy.

We sweat when we do intense workouts and excrete toxic substances from the body that would have otherwise been left inside the body. Sweating as a result of exercise is extremely healthy for our bodies.

5. Avoiding Stress.

Stress causes poor mental health. It is caused by the pressure to attain a certain threshold beyond our ability. We strain our minds and bodies when we push ourselves to the wall and we may eventually fall sick.

Poor mental health will catch up with our general health and if not taken care of early, it can irreversibly affect us.

6. Regular Health Check-Ups.

We should not go to the hospital only when we fall sick because it could be too late to save an already worse situation. We should visit a dentist bi-annually and an optician annually.

We should check our blood sugar levels and body pressure often to monitor any slight changes and address them before it is late. Good health is arrived at when we take care of all the variables affecting us.

7. Observing Health And Hygiene Standards.

There are health guidelines that are in place although hardly adhered to. They seem trivial but are very important in sustaining good health. We should not despise them.

Some guidelines are washing hands before meals and after visiting the toilet. We are also required to change our toothbrushes after every three months to promote dental hygiene.

8. Avoiding Self-Prescription Of Medicine.

It is common practice to buy medicine over the counter without a doctor's advice or prescription. It could have been prescribed to our friends or relatives and we think that we could also use it.

Doing this is wrong because there are many variables a medical officer considers before prescribing medicine that could not apply to us. Instead of getting well, we could worsen our health.

9. Do Not Share Medicine.

To ensure good health, do not share your medication with anyone without seeking professional advice. Not only could it not work for you, but you will also be endangering their health because you will tamper with their dosage.

Sharing of medicine could make you take expired medicine if the first person stopped taking it a long time ago and you use it without checking on the expiry date.

10. Understanding The Importance Of Good Health.

You only value what is important. When you understand the importance of good health, you will value it and observe that you do not lose it.

Health education is key to good health. Reading health literature and attending health talks will inspire you to work towards good health.

In conclusion, health is wealth. Take care of it early enough before it is unmanageable and costly.

Chapter 26:

6 Ways Your Emotions, Thoughts, and Behavior Contribute To What's Going On In Your Life

Emotions, thoughts, and behavior have an impact to compel us to do certain things in life. They control what we chose to do and what we don't. Sometimes it drives us to the significant ability to perceive and believe. It also forces us towards the outlook of the specific state of affairs. The emotion and thoughts we process while being conscious are easy to change and modify.

Somehow, emotions, thoughts, and behavior are interconnected with each other in a way or another. They depend on one another. The specific concept of an idea drives us towards a particular emotion. That emotion then leads us to the formation of different behaviors or actions. So, therefore, we can say that these turns on each other contribute to our lives. We depend on them on a daily basis.

1. The Benefits of Positive and Negative Emotions

We experience lots of emotions in our single life, either positive or negative. Positive emotion drives us to the more elite type of happiness, and it can make us aware of the bright side of everything. We feel light and satisfactory by almost the whole lot. Positive emotion opens our minds to more probability and prospects.

However, Negative emotions are just as important. The unconscious feeling of being alert and attentive saves us from trouble sometimes. But, a good balance of negative and positive emotions is needed in life to keep steadiness and right footing.

2. Emotion Intuition and Remembrance

A simple potion of positive emotion can encourage us to push ourselves more in some aspects of life, like studying for an exam or preparing for an interview. It can help us with the confidence of proving ourselves academically and educationally. The need to be successful and being on top comes with positive emotion to do so. It operates our intellect in such a way that we consider favorable outcomes in almost every facet. It intensifies the power of remembrance and enhancing our memory to a great extent. Even a negative emotion helps us to study because we become attentive due to the fear of losing or failing in that department. So, emotion does play an important role academically.

3. The Importance of Good Thoughts

We think about every action we imply beforehand. We are constantly analyzing everything in our brain before the consequence, even unconsciously sometimes. The thoughts drive us to specific behavior we carry out in our standard of living. As we have already imagined the outcome before the accurate results, we get a sense of comfort for what will happen. We become more relaxed and at ease. However, thinking too much or too excessively can be substandard for us and our mental health. Then over time, it becomes difficult to shut our mind when needed, which causes the formation of negative thoughts, which become, comparatively, more than the positive thoughts we had. Thus, we always need to relax our minds occasionally.

4. Thinking About Making The Decision

Making a decision can sometimes be a hard choice. The idea of choosing an option between two or more always seems quite strenuous. The fear of choosing the wrong or the comfort of choosing right comes with a great deal of moderate thought over the situation. So, we always give our thoughts a run at the circumstances, that what can be the outcome of a particular choice we are making in the process. Our thoughts constantly survey the position we are put into. We always get indecisive at some point, As it becomes difficult to concentrate on rights and wrongs. We would always need the thought of a master plan to a wiser choice.

5. The Welfare of Good Behavior

The behavior tells a lot about a person. Their personality depends upon the actions they manifest in daily life and all aspects of living. Good emotion and thought lead to good behavior. The action speaks louder than the words, so the behavior applied to the circumstance should be according to the requirement of the situation. It plays a vital role in daily life as we have to go through it daily to contribute to life. The power of influence nowadays is wielded like a weapon to build the strength of controlling specific points.

6. To Infuse Time and Energy

The public nowadays requires a working or waging method that uses the least amount of time and energy. Laziness has become a more prominent feature of society. A person's actions need more attention and energy to go through certain things, which makes it difficult for a person to ignore by time. There is a need to observe the gaps in certain situations and invest their time to get to the bottom of complex conditions. The men become determined to resolve such cases. It gives it all its time and energy to contribute to the simple necessities of life. And by the end of the day, the work can be done by multiple methods through observation.

Conclusion

Our emotions, thoughts, and behavior contribute in almost every way in our lives. Whether it be a positive thought, negative emotion, or excessive behavior, we always need them to complete our lifestyle by a large fraction. One impact each other, so the calculation to perform even a simple task needs work in these three aspects daily.

Chapter 27:

Keep Working When You're Just Not Feeling It

How many times in a day do you feel like doing nothing? How many times have you had the feeling of getting exhausted and have no energy or motivation to do anything? Do you want answers to these problems? Let's analyze some things.

What were the last big achievement that made you, your family, and your friends proud? When was the last time you had this urge to do a little more work just for the sake of it? Did you feel sorry for yourself and thought how tired you are? These are the problems! The things that don't make sense to you right now will become more meaningful and purposeful once you get out of your comfort zone. For that, you must start doing what you failed to do the last time.

These feelings of in-activeness and leisure are not a result of some circumstances but the inner voice of every human being that never sleeps and makes us feel like we cannot do this today. More than often, a change of self is needed than a change of the scenes surrounding us. This is the major task at hand that most people fail to achieve. But we can never give up. This is in fact the spirit of living. The spirit of keep going even when the hardest times hit.

Your body should be the easiest item for you to train and get a hold of. If you are not even able to do that, then there is very little hope for you to achieve anything ever again. So put yourself in motion and start creating. Instead of thinking about these wrong feelings that your heart gives out just to get you to sleep one more hour, use your time to get creative with life. You don't deserve a good sleep if you haven't done what was meant to be done today. You don't deserve a long breath of relaxation if you haven't tried hard enough to get out of this rut. You don't feel like getting the job done because you still have a sense of fear and self-pity that keeps you from giving your creative energies another try.

Human beings are the summary of what they repeatedly do, so excellence can also be a habit once you make changes in your behavior for it. If an inner voice tells you not to do something because you cannot do it, give it a trailer of what is about to come. You will get things done the very first time, and that voice will never bother you again.

These voices and feelings will make you procrastinate rather than performing those actions for real. This is no good way to use your creative energies, just to think of a beautiful scenario and not actually doing something to be in that scenario someday. And laying low because you don't feel like doing it today is the smallest hurdle to pass to get to that place.

All you need is some self-resilience and self-control and the ability to be the master of your body and I doubt there is anything that can stop you then.

Chapter 28:

8 Common Mistakes That Cause You to Make Bad Decisions

Are you too much of a perfectionist? Do you overestimate your abilities? Do you trust intuition too much? Are you overpowered by past decisions, even if they've been proven to be flawed? Let's hone in on ten mistakes we all make so that we may learn to stop tripping over the same stones repeatedly.

1. Holding Out For The Perfect Decision

Striving for perfection in our decisions adds unnecessary pressure and often leads to "analysis paralysis." No one likes to be wrong, but we must shake our fear and accept that decision-making means taking risks: sometimes we'll get it right, other times we won't. Mistakes are a part of learning.

"I've failed over and over and over again in my life. And that is why I succeed," boasts Michael Jordan, arguably the best basketball player of all time.

2. Failing To Face Reality

We tend to see things as we would like them to be, confusing wishful thinking with reality. For example, 75 percent of drivers think they are above average behind the wheel, which is statistically impossible.

Faced with a situation, we tend to take a stance and may fail to see beyond it, ignoring what might be better options out there. Furthermore, we tend to magnify the positive aspects of our stance and minimize the negative ones. One good way to avoid this bias is to try and distinguish facts (objective) from opinions (subjective).

3. Falling For Self-Deceptions

The way we are presented with a situation, and the way we present it to ourselves, affects our final decisions. For example, when some cancer patients were told that the survival rate one year after surgery was 68 percent, a significant percentage opted for that surgery. Meanwhile, when others were told that 32 percent of patients die within a year of the operation, no one elected to undergo it. The same information was given, just presented differently.

To avoid falling prey to self-deception, it is important to seek alternatives and consider them from different angles. Finally, sleep on it before making the decision.

4. Going With The Flow

There is something worse than being wrong: being the only one who is wrong. Doing what everyone else does is easier and, more importantly, may save us from embarrassment. Hence our tendency to follow the herd, even if it is heading to a precipice.

We saw this with the dot-com bubble, for example. Everyone wanted to invest in tech companies when the bubble inflated, even when most investors knew little about them.

The problem with imitation (and not thinking before deciding) is that we eliminate the possibility of finding wiser alternatives than what is fashionable.

5. Rushing and Risking Too Much

Before deciding hastily, we should consider whether a decision is truly urgent. We tend to rush into things, crossing things off our list to feel accomplished. But all we're doing in a rush is taking unnecessary risks.

For example, the Chernobyl disaster was caused by an unnecessary test that simulated a power failure at the nuclear power plant. The outcome was exactly what they sought to avoid by going through the motions for security testing: the reactor exploded. There was no urgent need to run that test, but it happened anyway, risking far too much.

6. Relying Too Heavily on Intuition

Intuition can be an asset, but it leads to mistakes when we allow it to outweigh analytical thinking. What's more, testing our hunches with low-cost experiments is important.

The authors offer Samsung chairman Lee Kun-hee as a cautionary tale. In the 1990s, he reportedly decided to get into automobile manufacturing because he "sensed" the market would take off in Asia. The project resulted in a loss of $2 billion and 50,000 layoffs.

7. Being Married To Our Ideas

It's hard for us to change a prior decision, even if keeping the status quo is inefficient or harmful.

The year 2003 saw the grounding of the Concorde, a supersonic jet airliner that was never profitable. But it took a fatal accident, with over 100 fatalities, to put it into permanent retirement. Economically speaking, the right decision should have been made long before then, but that meant acknowledging a failure. And no one likes doing that.

8. Paying Little Heed to Consequences

Sometimes we don't consider the consequences of a decision. Or we only consider the most direct and immediate ones, ignoring the side effects. And that can cause even bigger problems than the ones we were trying to solve in the first place.

That's what happened to those in charge of the Titanic, who wanted to arrive at their destination 24 hours ahead of schedule to silence critics who claimed their large ship would be slow. They ignored warnings about icebergs, warnings that should have slowed them down for safety's sake.

Chapter 29:

Don't Live Your Life In Regret

Take this for a lesson today; There is no greater pain than that of regret.

Hopelessness is one thing that can crack a soul, but nothing is more hurting than that of lifelong regret. We take up things in our life that we deem helpful for the times to come. But never do we ever take risks, just because we want to have a smooth uncomplicated life.

Life was never meant to be lived as reading off a paper. Neither can you expect it to be a smooth walk on a beach? There are always some pebbles on the way and always some hedges where you need to twist and turn to fit and climb.

We all will eventually o through a period of endless questioning where we judge our every step and every decision whether if it was bad or not good enough!

But why are we indulging in this waste of time when we have so much better things to do right now in this present time slot.

When you are on a long journey, nothing will make sense. When you are on your path to greatness, you will always look back and get drawn back a little every time.

But once you reach the top, you will have a final look back into your past and everything will make sense in a split second.

Life is a roller coaster and we all have baggage. We must have because no one can have lived a long life and have a straight, plain, and colorless script where nothing happened out of the ordinary.

The uncertainty of life is what defines life to its true reality.

We, humans, are a combination of deterministic and non-deterministic behavior where we get triggered on thoughts of shame and failure but rarely do we learn to listen to those failures and try to change our habits.

Things have a course of happening and we always get behind the things that take most of us down the lane. That is where we feel the walk of shame and remember the feeling for the rest of our life.

But why do we feel the urge to remain connected to our shameful past? What needs do we have with feeling shame? Why do we need to remember and regret the things that the world has forgotten a long time ago? Why do we need to keep those memories alive?

A billion incidents are happening every second and we try to keep all our baggage with us till the day we take it with us to our graves.

What we should be doing is to forgive everyone and especially ourselves, to release some positive energy and make some space for the happy times that are to come.

We should let those happy moments erase all our regrets and ease our path for the best future that time could ever earn us. But what you should do ultimately, is to regret what you haven't done yet, rather than what you have done!

Chapter 30:

Motivation With Good Feelings

Ever wonder what goes on in your mind when you feel depressed isn't always the reaction to the things that happen to you? What you go through when you feel down is the chemistry of your brain that you yourself allow being created in the first place.

You don't feel weak just because your heart feels so heavy. You feel weak because you have filled your heart with all these feelings that don't let you do something useful.

Feelings are not your enemy till you choose the wrong ones. In fact, Feelings and emotions can be the strongest weapon to have in your arsenal.

People say, "You are a man, so act like one. Men don't cry, they act strong and brave"

You must make yourself strong enough to overcome any feelings of failure or fear. Any thought that makes you go aloof and dims that light of creativity and confidence. It's OK to feel sad and cry for some time, but it's not OK to feel weak for even a second.

Your consciousness dictates your feelings. Your senses help you to process a moment and in turn help you translate them into feelings that go both ways. This process has been going on from the day you were born and will continue till your last day.

You enter your consciousness as soon as you open your eyes to greet the day. It is at this moment when your creativity is at its peak. What you need now is just a set of useful thoughts and emotions that steer your whole day into a worthwhile one.

Don't spend your day regretting and repressing things you did or someone else did to you. You don't need these feelings right now. Because you successfully passed those tests of life and are alive still to be grateful for what you have right now.

There are a billion things in life to be thankful for and a billion more to be sad for. But you cannot live a happy fulfilling life if you focus on the later ones.

Life is too short to be sad and to be weak. When you start your day, don't worry about what needs to be done. But think about who you need to be to get those things done.
Don't let actions and outcomes drive you. Be the sailor of yourself to decide what outcomes you want.

Believe me, the feeling of gratitude is the biggest motivator. Self gratitude should be the level of appraisal to expect. Nothing should matter after your own opinions about yourself.

If you let other people's opinions affect your feelings, you are the weakest person out there. And failure is your destination.

Visualization of a better life can help you feel and hope better. It would help you to grow stronger and faster but remember; The day you lose control of your emotions, feelings, and your temper, your imagination will only lead you to a downward spiral.

Chapter 31:

Five Ways To Control Your Thoughts

The power of thoughts.

Thoughts are very powerful because they greatly influence the direction our lives take. Our failures and successes are anchored on our thinking patterns. We score big in life when we learn how to dominate our minds and submit them to our desires.

The greater the external influence on our decisions, the more likely we lose control of our thoughts. Here are five ways to control your thoughts:

1. Meditation.

It is the ability to reflect deeply on the occurrences in your life. Meditation is taking a deep reflective introspect of your life. Sometimes we need to take a break from our busy schedules and look back at the far we have come from. The journey we have walked hitherto shall inspire us to confidently move into the future.

Meditation is often perceived as old-fashioned because it is very basic. It appears unattractive but once you learn to do it in the right way, there is no turning back. Do not mistake it for idleness or wishful thinking because it is neither of them.

It begins with a mental walk down memory lane. You count your blessings one after another and take stock of your achievements. You can consolidate your thoughts through meditation as you plan for your next move. Meditation provides room for mental growth because you are free from any pressure to act therein.

2. <u>Taking feedback.</u>

How is feedback related to controlling our thoughts? There is a strong connection between the two. We live in a social world where interaction with different types of people is inevitable. Their perceptions and the doctrines they believe also vary. The people we live amongst are the mirror in which we can look at ourselves.

Strangers, friends, and family are very important circles that we surround ourselves with. Apart from strangers, our family and friends have been with us long enough to understand our thinking patterns. Their feedback about our decisions on various issues is very important because we can control our thoughts bordering on their suggestions.

We should learn to take feedback even from strangers we interact with briefly. They could make very important observations on our intellectuality which could spell the turning point of our thoughts. The power of feedback should not be underrated.

3. <u>Taking a SWOT analysis.</u>

We may have considered a SWOT analysis on our businesses but not on ourselves. If it is good for business, why is it not for ourselves? Our thoughts need to be audited from time to time for us to identify the red flags within. We can thereafter act from a point of knowledge because we understand our strengths and weaknesses even better.

We can work to improve our weaknesses and fortify our strengths in thoughts when we analyze them thoroughly. We can program our thoughts when we understand our personalities better.

A SWOT analysis enables us to identify the red zones we should not enter because they could spell doom for us. We also learn the limits we should not exceed because they threaten to disrupt our good thoughts. We operate within a healthy framework that our minds flourish.

4. Submitting to spiritual authority.

It is good to subscribe to a belief or religion. Every religion has its practices that are beyond physical comprehension if your heart and thoughts are left out. The beauty of religious beliefs is its mystery in understanding the spirituality concepts around them.

Religion reinforces morality and upright thinking. Religious people train their thoughts within the confines of their beliefs. This enables them to be disciplined and control their thoughts not to stray away from the values they practice.

Religion rebukes evil thoughts and promotes the good ones. It is the prefect of upright thinking and curbs many evils before they even happen. If you have a problem with having your thoughts under control, consider joining a religion.

5. Consider the fear of the unknown.

Fear is destructive when misused but very constructive when channeled correctly. The fear of the unknown is a limiting factor to very many things. Over the years, humanity has restrained itself from acting or thinking against acceptable societal norms because of the fear of the unknown that lies beyond.

You can bring your thoughts to submission when you consider the red zones that you should not approach, even in your mind. Your thinking will be disciplined not to stray into unchartered territories because of untold consequences.

In conclusion, controlling our thoughts is a big win if we at all want to be successful. These five ways are effective in bringing your thoughts to submission.

Chapter 32:

Five Habits We Consider Harmless

Familiarity breeds contempt. There are habits that we have become so accustomed to that hinder us from achieving our full potential. We consider them little and insignificant in our lives. Sometimes, we go to the extremes of defending ourselves when we are corrected and advised to abandon them. It is a sad state to be in and one that requires enlightenment and self-awareness to be able to get out of that quagmire. Here are five habits that we consider harmless:

1. Blue Screen Addiction

Blue screen addiction is the addiction to digital media and video games. This is a common problem, especially for millennials. It is often considered inconsequential, a myth that has been debunked by real-life experiences.

Most people spend a lot of time working through their computers, using their mobile phones or tablets, playing video games, or watching television. The use of digital media in this era is almost unavoidable. Regardless of this digital evolution, there have been some excesses. Heavy use of these devices has broken the social code since most people can only communicate through communication apps and not physically. Faceless cyberbullies have attacked and trolled innocent netizens and ruined their reputation.

News spread fast via the internet and it is not a surprise that addiction to blue screens is on the rise. It is not as harmless as it may seem and its effects are long-lasting.. It causes poor eyesight and sometimes migraines.

2. Procrastination

It is the habit of postponing tasks to be done presently to a later time. Most people relate to this habit that has grown roots in our lifestyle. Before you judge yourself harshly for doing this, statistics have it that over 80% of college students engage in procrastination and it has chronically affected at least 20% of adults. That is just the tip of the iceberg.

We comfort ourselves that we are not alone in this ocean that has drowned the ambitions and potential of many people. We err in finding comfort in this well-dressed misery of procrastination. It is not as harmless as it superficially looks.

Procrastination encourages laziness which has, in turn, made many people pay a higher price for engaging in it. Some have lost their employment for leaving incomplete tasks at work, others have missed out on promotions for incompetence and a further group has failed to secure business opportunities that required their attention at the opportune time when they had put everything on hold. What is the cost we are ready to pay for in procrastination?

We should sober up and abandon procrastination by acting on matters that need our immediate attention. Shelving our response for a later time causes more harm than good.

3. Making Obnoxious Jokes

There is a limit to the extreme one can go when making jokes. It should never go overboard to hurt the feelings of our friends and associates. Many times we underestimate or maybe do not consider the impact our words may have on our friends and those around us. We unknowingly hurt their self-esteem and they feel worthless after what turns out to be a bad joke. We should always know when to stop and apologize for our excesses because we never know how much we have hurt our friends when we make bad jokes about them.

It is inconsiderate of us not to take into account the struggles of our friends when we make fun of their situation. It seems harmless but has the potential to completely cut off one's dreams.

4. Building A Fortress

The single greatest mistake that we unknowingly commit is building a fortress for ourselves to hide from the rest of the world. Indeed, the world can sometimes be cruel and unforgiving, making us run to the nearest point of safety. We build walls instead of bridges to separate us from the harsh reality. This solution is short-lived because the fortress will cut you off from the rest of the world.

You will live in solitude without any news and over time your resources will be depleted. The fortress may not necessarily be physical but also social. As much as introverts manage to keep off squabbles and fights, they lack a network to connect. It is not safe to be alone in this ever-changing world. Find a person or group with whom you share common interests and build a network.

Your network is your net worth.

5. Glossing Over Facts

Facts should be the language you speak. We often omit or ignore facts that we deem irrelevant to us but surprisingly turn out to be very important. When you get your facts right, everything falls into place. Often, the average person does not go into the details. Remember the devil lies in the details? It is therein where you will find solutions to matters that you overlooked.

Stand out by grasping correct facts about a matter before you indulge in them. It is harmful not to be aware of your surroundings or get your facts right because it puts your competence on the relevant subject matter in question.

You should check out these five habits that we mistakenly consider harmless and adjust your approach.

Chapter 33:

10 Habits of Selena Gomez

Selena Gomez is one of the sweetest celebrities you'll ever meet, and at just 29 years old, she never ceases to amaze. She has amassed a large following on all platforms with her outstanding talent, personality, and wholesome beauty! Selena is an American songwriter, singer, actress, executive producer, cooking show host, founder, and owner of the 'Rare Beauty.'

Her albums always chart at the top of the US charts, and most of all, she's won several awards, including World Guinness Records and many more. Selena has had her share of struggles from being diagnosed with Lupus, to going through a very public breakup, but has remained stronger than ever.

Here are 10 habits of Selena Gomez you can steal from.

1. Love Yourself

Selena Gomez believes in putting herself first above anything else. In an interview with NPR's Lulu Garcia-Navarro, she discussed her body image issues. She admitted being overweight and body-shamed, her kidney transplant being ridiculed, and her very public breakup with Justin Bieber. As she says, "don't allow yourself to sink; instead, believe in yourself, in your inner capabilities, and don't allow the hate to overwhelm you."

2. She Goes to Therapy

Sometimes you'll have to talk it all out to be a completely ready self-aware person. Selena, whose beauty business 'Rare Beauty donates a portion of its proceeds to promoting mental health access, spoke to Vogue Australia about how her therapy treatment molded her into the person she is now.

3. Kill Them With Kindness

Treat your haters with kindness, as battling anger with range is futile. Selena Gomez has dwelt with trolls and bullies, both online and in person-from being called out for her weight to being criticized for Lupus, kidney transplant, and some calling her out as a "weak vocalist." She continually tries not to be bothered by it and teaches her fans to be kind. "Your falsehoods are bullets, your voice is a gun, and no war in rage was ever won," she sings in a song from her Revival album. This suggests that your words have power and may impact people's lives positively or negatively.

4. Take a Break if Need Be

Being a major voice in the entertainment industry is not for the faint-hearted; take a break when necessary. Gomez understands the value of taking breaks, which allows her to reconnect with herself, her body, and her priorities. And when you have millions of followers, any setback can affect your entire existence for eternity.

5. Keep Strong

For Selena, remaining strong is ideally the way to approach life to avoid taking advantage of her. To stay strong, you'll have to maintain mental and physical positivism. And to achieve this, do things that keep you motivated and happy, no matter how tiny or big they are.

6. Starts the Day With a Positive Attitude

If your first thought when the alarm clock goes off is degrading or harsh, you're setting the tone for a negative attitude for the rest of the day. Gomez explained on Instagram live that to stay positive; she read a book called Jesus Calling every morning.

7. Girl Power

Selena Gomez has maintained close friendships with other women in the industry, including her best friend, Taylor Swift. In 2016, their friendship was frequently referred to as "squad goals." The support they portrayed to each other. You'll gain when you keep closing those who make you happy and suffer in the hands of those with pessimistic or narrow mind-set.

8. Heartbreak keeps happening

Selena, like anybody else, has experienced the gut-wrenching agony of being hurt. It's not easy, and it's certainly not entertaining for anyone. Selena is here to let you that such experiences are perfect learning opportunities. After all, everything happens for a reason.

9. Give Back

Giving back not only brings you joy but also helps you develop a stronger sense of self. Selena is designated a UNICEF Ambassador, but she has also traveled the world to make a difference in places such as Ghana, Kenya, and Nepal. She has also collaborated with WE Day.

10. Humility

Selena is a good example of "if down-to-earth" as a person. Her humility is always genuine and persistent. You don't always have to depict yourself as fancy and showy for people to like you in life.

Conclusion

If you need to make a bold step in your life, career, or any other aspect of your life, feel inspired by Selena Gomez's actions or habits. Because standing up for yourself will almost probably motivate someone else to take the courageous action required.

Chapter 34:

10 Habits of Jennifer Lawrence

Jennifer Lawrence is one of Hollywood's most famous actress, thanks to her role in films such as "The Hunger Games" and "Silver Linings Playbook." But, before her tremendous success, Lawrence struggled to build a name for herself as an actress and model in New York, where she moved when she was 14 years old. After breaking out as the tough-as-nails teenager Ree in the 2010 indie drama "Winter's Bone," Lawrence went on to star in multiple "X-Men" films and drama such as "American Hustle."

I can't think of anyone who doesn't adore Jennifer Lawrence. What is it about this actress that makes her so appealing? It's easy to list a thousand reasons to admire Jennifer Lawrence -from her incredible skill to her quick-witted humour- but honestly, the life lessons she attracts everyone to her.

Here are 10 life habits that Lawrence offers as lessons simply by being herself.

1. Strive for Health and Strength

"I'm never going to starve myself for a part," she declared on the cover of Elle in December 2012. "I don't want little girls to think, 'Oh, I want to look like Katniss; hence I'll skip meals." When you're trying to get your physique to appear just suitable, Emma on the other end is trying to make her body appear muscular and robust rather than skinny.

2. Refresh Yourself

How many times has Lawrence stumbled? That's what probably comes to your mind every time you see her trip over the hem of her gown at an awards presentation. Can anyone blame the girl for this? Those outfits appear to be impossible to walk in! But she trips, and every time, without fail, she gets back up and continues walking.

3. Accept Responsibility for Your Mistakes

Lawrence's awkward moments are all the more endearing because she is always the first to laugh at how clumsy she is when she stands. Remember when she collapsed at the 2013 Academy Awards? Or when she collapsed on the red carpet of the 2014 Academy Awards? What does it matter? We're all human, and J. Law never tries to hide it by acting cool and so should you.

4. The Truth Will Set You Free

Even if your truth seems to hurt more, such as that you pee very quickly or that your breasts are unequal, J. Law says that it is what it is, and to be anything other than herself isn't allowed. Embrace your flaws!

5. Look Past the Hype

Remember to key in what's genuine and what's not, and to keep your things in perspective, look past those who take themselves too seriously.

6. Maintain An Open Mind

Lawrence told E! News that her acting job will not bind her for the rest of her life. However, she understands that things happen and that people's lives change, and she is prepared to keep an open mind about it. Being open-minded will direct you to break the monotony for future possibilities.

7. Nobody Is Flawless

Can you recall a scene in American Hustle in which Lawrence's character discusses nail polish? Do you remember the nail polish? She claims it's the smell that keeps drawing her back since it's delicious on the outside but rotten on the inside. Not only is it a beautiful moment, but the discussion is a metaphor for everyone's good and evil sides. Nobody is flawless, and no one loves it when others claim to be.

8. Humility

During a BBC Radio 1 interview, Lawrence remarked her involvement in "The Hunger Games," where she genuinely adores watching the movies she makes because she gets to see how much of a troll, bad, and untalented is. Weird! Indeed, you wouldn't agree with her right? Bu she's adorable because she is humble.

9. Maintain a Sense of Humour

During an interview with Vogue, Lawrence sense of humour could be seen when she cracked a joke on how seeing 13-year olds give her nightmares. She effortlessly doesn't take life too seriously.

10. Love Your Body

Lawrence has spoken out numerous times about her body, challenging unrealistic beauty standards. She claimed in an interview with FLARE magazine that she would rather appear overweight on camera (and appear normal) than diet only to dress like a scarecrow. That is a whole lot of body positivity just for you!

Conclusion

Jennifer will teach you profound truths- when she acts, and when she put on a mask that conceals who she truly is. She given up none of her power by leaving the covers on the screen and refusing to act to "fit in" with Hollywood culture.

Chapter 35:

10 habits of Beyoncé

Beyonce is a renowned Houston-born singer, dancer, songwriter, actor, and businesswoman. She rose to prominence as a member of the pop singing R&B group "Destiny's Child." Beyonce is ultimately life goals; she is always at the top of her game, tries new things (and smashes them), admits her mistakes, balances her family life, and spends time with the people who matter. She always points out on working tirelessly to the top with the help of her mother and father from the age of nine.

How has she managed to win Grammys, make platinum albums, star in many A-list films, run a lucrative clothing line, perfume business, and raising three gorgeous children?

Here are 10 Mrs. Carter habits that you can emulate.

1. Above All, Love Yourself

Beyonce have had a share of work-family balance struggles when raising her three kids. Realizing how overwhelming it can be, she opts for self-love practices that means more rest if need be. You have goals and desires, which is terrific! But it's pointless making all that only to die as soon as you acquire it. Practise self-care.

2. Make the Most of Your Time

Beyonce's advice as a self-made millionaire is not to waste time. If you want to attain your goals, you must respect your time before others do.

Everyone, rich or poor, has the same number of hours in a day. But the question is, what are you doing with your 24 hours? Are you making the best use of your time?

3. Keep Your Personal Life a Mystery

Talking to Oprah in an interview, "Queen Bey" said that she is purposefully private because revealing everything deprives her of enjoying her personal life. Your personal life should be sacred because letting everyone in may ruin it.

Beyonce believes that he fans should only be familiar with her through her art and music; the rest she reserves for her family and friends.

4. Love Your Body

Beyoncé is a representation of beauty, power, and health. Beyoncé recently claimed that she has been following a vegan diet, not for weight loss, but to be the best version of herself. Spending time on yourself is crucial, and learning to love yourself is imperative, whether the healthiest version of yourself means giving up meat or simply spending an extra few hours in the gym each month.

5. Be the Best Version of You

If there is one thing we can learn from Beyonce, is that no one will scold you on bringing out your best. Quoting her words in her documentary, "power will never be given to you; you must take it yourself." If you want it big, nobody is going to do it for you. If you are not invited to the table, drag yourself a chair and sit.

6. Take Charge of Your Success

Beyonce is a good example of what economic equality is. She is one who doesn't shy off celebrating her achievements as a woman. Beyonce isn't afraid to flaunt her "paper" and personal accomplishments. She is always proud of her hustle and isn't afraid to exploit her past triumphs to prove her worth. That is how you advance - both professionally and personally.

7. Hard Work Is Recognizable

A "smart person" will frequently imply that good soft skills can compensate for time spent on "the little things." However, Beyonce's stage appearance and performance demonstrates that hard work will be appreciated by those who admire your work, as well as those who don't know you.

8. Opinionated

Beyonce is defined by her beauty and brains. She is an activist on important topics, for instant, her opinions had an influence during Obama's administration, and she also promoted Michelle Obama's efforts to promote humanitarianism. Weigh in your opinion where it matters.

9. Negativity Derails You

Stay away from negativity and concentrate on working hard and doing your best. Beyonce is a challenge to most of her peers in the industry because she does not waste time on frivolous things and the negative people on her pages trying to bring her.

10. Her Priorities

Beyoncé's story revolves around her family, and she frequently emphasizes it as her driving force. Those people who journey with you from scratch to success are the same people who you should credit.

Conclusion

There is nothing powerful than knowing and respecting your worth as well as remaining solid on your money-making journey. Even if you don't have Beyoncé's level of riches, learn to handle your life cautiously.

CPSIA information can be obtained
at www.ICGtesting.com
Printed in the USA
LVHW081959130122
708314LV00013B/575